AFRICAN BUFFALO

AFRICAN ANIMAL DISCOVERY LIBRARY

Lynn M. Stone

Rourke Corporation, Inc.
Vero Beach, Florida 32964

PHOTO CREDITS

All photos by the Author

LIBRARY OF CONGRESS
Library of Congress Cataloging-in-Publication Data
Stone, Lynn M.
  African Buffalo / by Lynn M. Stone.

    p. cm. — (African animal discovery library)
    Summary: An introduction to the physical characteristics,
habits, and natural environment of the two species of African
buffalo that can be found in many parts of Africa below the
Sahara Desert.
    ISBN 0-86593-052-X
    1. African Buffalo—Juvenile literature. [1. African buffalo.]
I. Title. II. Series: Stone, Lynn M. African animal discovery
library.
QL737.U53S74   1990
599.73'58—dc20   89-48434
                                        CIP
                                        AC

African buffalo

TABLE OF CONTENTS

THE AFRICAN BUFFALO

African buffalo *(Syncerus caffer)* are big, cow-like animals. They have deep chests and thick shoulders. Old males, the buffalo **bulls,** can weigh nearly 2,000 pounds.

The bulls have wide, sweeping horns and a "helmet" on their foreheads. The "helmet" covers the bull's forehead. It's made of horn, and it joins the two sharp horns on either side.

Hunters tell stories of being charged by buffalo bulls. All of the stories may not be true, but a man on foot is no match for an African Buffalo.

Buffalo bull

THE BUFFALO'S COUSINS

The African buffalo is related to all the **cud** chewing animals—antelope, bison, goats, sheep, and cattle. Like these animals, African buffalo graze on grass and chew a cud. A cud is the food that is eaten quickly and later pumped up from the stomach for more chewing.

Four other kinds of buffalo live in Asia. The "buffalo" of the United States and Canada is really a **bison.** It is much shaggier than the buffalo, and it has a different shape.

American bison bull

HOW THEY LOOK

African buffalo show differences in size and color. Still, they are all the same basic animal.

The buffalo of the grasslands in East Africa are much larger than the buffalo of African forests. Big buffalo stand nearly six feet tall at the shoulder.

African buffalo may be black, brown, or reddish-brown. Where a buffalo lives usually decides its color. Buffalo of the grasslands are black.

Both males and females have horns. Bulls have heavier horns than the females, or **cows.**

Buffalo bull

WHERE THEY LIVE

The African buffalo lives in many parts of Africa south of the hot, dry Sahara Desert.

Buffalo are fond of water. They like to splash, wallow, and soak. They also like to eat plants that grow in and near water, and they like to drink. A buffalo may drink 10 gallons of water in a day.

Buffalo have many homes. They may be found in forests, swamps, brush, and grassland. Some wander high into mountains.

Buffalo herd

Buffalo herd

HOW THEY LIVE

African buffalo are active early in the morning and in the evening. They feed at these times. They rest and chew their cuds during the warmest part of the day.

Buffalo are not usually noisy, but fighting bulls sometimes bellow. Calves make loud, mooing calls. Buffalo also grunt.

Most buffalo live together in groups called **herds.** Old males, however, often live by themselves.

After age 10, bulls are usually driven away from the herd by younger, stronger bulls.

Oxpeckers on buffalo cow

THE BUFFALO'S CALVES

A buffalo cow usually has one calf. She rarely has twins.

Calves are reddish-brown. They weigh up to 90 pounds at birth. Their hair is much thicker and more wool-like than an adult buffalo's.

Female calves may stay with their mothers until they have calves of their own. Buffalo have calves when they are four or five.

Young males leave their mothers when they are two. They join herds of other bulls.

Buffalo in the wild can live to be at least 20. Captives have reached 29.

Buffalo calf

PREDATOR AND PREY

Buffalo are plant-eaters. Plant-eating animals are the **prey,** or food, of meat-eating animals.

The meat-eating animals that feed on buffalo are called **predators.** The most dangerous predator to buffalo is the lion.

Lions take a risk when they attack a big buffalo. An angry buffalo's horns and feet can kill a lion.

Packs of spotted hyenas are predators of young buffalo.

Buffalo have a keen sense of smell. But their eyes and ears are only fair.

Lion eating buffalo

BUFFALO AND PEOPLE

An animal's **range** is the whole area in which it lives. The African buffalo used to live in many more places than it does now. Its range has become smaller.

Buffalo have been hunted too much. People have shot them for their horns and meat.

Buffalo are moody animals. It is hard to tell what a buffalo will do next. People usually avoid walking too close to African buffalo.

Buffalo bull
Mara Game Reserve

THE BUFFALO'S FUTURE

Thousands of African buffalo still live in two East African nations, Kenya and Tanzania. In most other African countries, buffalo are no longer common.

African buffalo need huge pieces of wild land for their homes. The wild land of Africa is disappearing. More land is being used for people's homes and for growing the food that people eat.

In the future wildlife parks may be the buffalo's only homes.

Glossary

bison (BI sun)—a huge, horned, cud-chewing mammal with wooly hair; found only in North America and Europe

bull (BUHL)—a male buffalo, bison, or other large, hoofed mammal

cow (KOW)—a female buffalo, bison, or other large, hoofed mammal

cud (KUHD)—food which is chewed a second time after already having been chewed and swallowed once

herd (HERD)—a group of large, hoofed animals, such as buffalo

predator (PRED a tor)—an animal that kills another animal for food

prey (PREY)—an animal that is hunted by another animal for food

range (RAYNGE)—the entire area in which a certain type of animal lives

INDEX